M000195171

TO:

FROM:

Zen

Compiled by
Suzanne Schwalb
and Jax Berman

 PETER PAUPER PRESS, INC.
White Plains, New York

Designed by Margaret Rubiano

Copyright © 2015

Peter Pauper Press, Inc.

202 Mamaroneck Avenue

White Plains, NY 10601

ISBN 978-1-4413-1830-5

Printed in China

7 6 5 4 3 2 1

Visit us at www.peterpauper.com

Zen

INTRODUCTION

Zen is a practice: The practice of the art of living. Through Zen, one seeks to "Be here now," to do without hesitation, to live in the moment, to free one's spirit from obstacles and distractions. *Zen*, or *Chan* in Chinese, comprises the Chinese traditions of Buddhism with those of other Asian cultures, especially Japan.

Buddha is a title meaning "awakened one." The original Buddha was Siddhartha Gautama, a prince from the present-day country of Nepal; upon his personal awakening more than twenty-five hundred years ago, he sought to share *dharma* (teaching) with others. A thousand years later, Bodhidharma brought the practice to China, and it arrived in Japan six centuries thereafter. The word *Zen* is a Japanese word. Like *Chan*, it is derived from the Sanskrit word *dhyana*, meaning "meditation."

In this mercurial world, it may be difficult to achieve mindfulness and far too easy to lose the Zen sense of self. Let this little tea-table tribute keep you company with its medley of samplings from sages East and West. May these proverbs, haikus, quotes, and koans* provide a bit of zenspiration for your journey.

Be here now.

*A koan is a statement, story, or question intended to impel one to put aside reason and gain intuitive insight.

6/7/17

Knock on the
sky and listen
to the sound!

ZEN KOAN

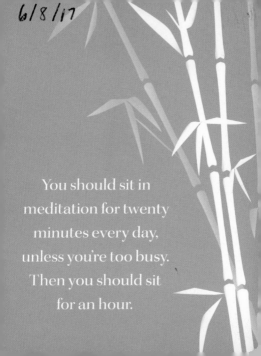

6/8/17

You should sit in
meditation for twenty
minutes every day,
unless you're too busy.
Then you should sit
for an hour.

Be empty of worrying. Think of who created thought!

RUMI

6/10/17

If I keep a green
bough in my heart,
the singing bird
will come.

CHINESE PROVERB

6/11/17

Poppy petals fall
Softly quietly calmly
When they are ready.

ETSUJIN

There is more
to life than
increasing its
speed.

GANDHI

Happiness is simple. Everything we do to find it is complicated.

KAREN MAEZEN MILLER

Each morning we are born again. What we do today is what matters most.

JACK KORNFIELD

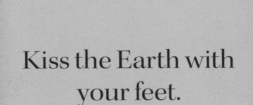

Kiss the Earth with
your feet.

Thích Nhất Hanh

The truth knocks on the door and you say, "Go away, I'm looking for the truth," and so it goes away. Puzzling.

ROBERT M. PIRSIG,
*Zen and the Art of
Motorcycle Maintenance*

True change is within. Leave the outside as it is.

DALAI LAMA

Drop by drop is the water pot filled.

BUDDHA

Sitting quietly,
doing nothing,
spring comes,
and the grass
grows by itself.

ZEN PROVERB

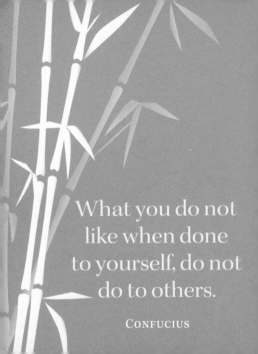

What you do not
like when done
to yourself, do not
do to others.

CONFUCIUS

Chanting at
the altar
Of the inner
sanctuary...
A cricket priest.

ISSA

Our heads
are round so
thought can
change direction.

FRANCIS PICABIA

Your work is
to discover your
world and then
with all your heart
give yourself to it.

Roaring dreams
take place
in a perfectly
silent mind.

JACK KEROUAC

Move and the way will open.

ZEN PROVERB

Each man had only one genuine vocation—to find his way to himself.

HERMAN HESSE

You, yourself, as
much as anybody in
the entire universe,
deserve your love
and affection.

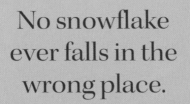

No snowflake
ever falls in the
wrong place.

ZEN PROVERB

Riverbank
plum tree …
Do your reflected
blossoms
Really flow away?

BUSON

Peace comes
from within. Do not
seek it without.

You are the sky.
Everything else—
it's just
the weather.

PEMA CHÖDRÖN

To see a World
in a Grain of Sand
And a Heaven in
a Wild Flower,
Hold Infinity in the
palm of your hand
And Eternity in an hour.

WILLIAM BLAKE

Be happy for
this moment.
This moment
is your life.

Omar Khayyám

Be grateful for
whoever comes,
because each has
been sent as a guide
from beyond.

RUMI

The most difficult times for many of us are the ones we give ourselves.

PEMA CHÖDRÖN

Remember that
not getting what
you want is
sometimes a
wonderful stroke
of luck.

H. JACKSON BROWN, JR.

When the student is ready, the Master appears.

MABEL COLLINS

Stop acting
so small. You are the
universe in
ecstatic motion.

RUMI

I have never listened to anyone who criticized my taste in space travel, sideshows, or gorillas. When this occurs, I pack up my dinosaurs and leave the room.

RAY BRADBURY

Before enlightenment,
chop wood, carry water.
After enlightenment,
chop wood, carry water.

ZEN PROVERB

To a mind that
is still, the whole
universe surrenders.

LAO TZU

He did each single thing, as if he did nothing else.

CHARLES DICKENS

To what shall I
liken the world?
Moonlight reflected
in dewdrops,
Shaken from a
crane's bill.

DOGEN

If you light
a lamp for
someone else,
it will also
brighten your
own path.

NICHIREN DAISHONEN

You know the
sound of two
hands clapping.
Tell me, what is
the sound of
one hand?

HAKUIN EKAKU

During a meditation retreat, a student asked Soen Nakagawa, "I am very discouraged. What should I do?" Soen replied, "Encourage others."

If you're
feeling helpless,
help someone.

Aung San Suu Kyi

If you want to climb a mountain, begin at the top.

ZEN KOAN

Every living
being is an
engine geared
to the wheelwork
of the universe.

NIKOLA TESLA

When walking just
walk. When sitting
just sit. Above all,
don't wobble.

ZEN PROVERB

Time is not a line,
but a series of now
points.

TAISEN DESHIMARU

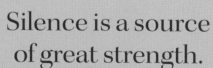

Silence is a source
of great strength.

LAO TZU

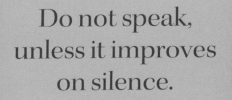

Do not speak,
unless it improves
on silence.

BUDDHIST PROVERB

The obstacle is the path.

ZEN PROVERB

One day a student asked Taiga, "What is the most difficult part of painting?" Taiga answered, "The part of the paper where nothing is painted is the most difficult."

Spring night—
one hour worth
a thousand
gold coins.

SU TONG-P'O

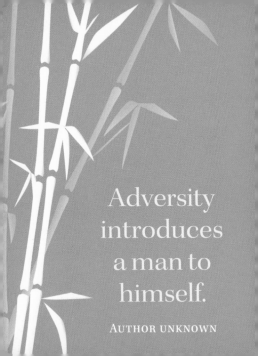

Adversity
introduces
a man to
himself.

AUTHOR UNKNOWN

The sound
of water says
what I think.

ZHUANGZI

The moon
abiding in the
midst of
serene mind;
billows break
into light.

DOGEN

My admonition
is this: Be a
Great Fool!
A petty little fool
is nothing but a
worldling. But a
Great Fool is
a Buddha!

HARADA-ROSHI

Fallen now to earth
After dancing
journeyings ...
Kite that lost
its soul.

Kubonta

If we wonder
often, the gift
of knowledge
will come.

ARAPAHO SAYING

He who asks
a question is a fool
for five minutes;
he who does not
ask remains a
fool forever.

CHINESE PROVERB

Feelings come
and go like clouds
in a windy sky.
Conscious breathing
is my anchor.

THÍCH NHẤT HẠNH

A student approached the Master and said, "Please, Master, I am lost. I feel I don't know who I am. Show me my true self!" But the Master would not answer and looked away. The student begged, to no avail, and at last decided to leave. At that moment the Master called him by name. "Yes!" replied the student, turning. "There it is!" said the Master.

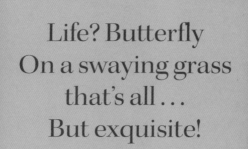

Life? Butterfly
On a swaying grass
that's all …
But exquisite!

SOIN

Man stands in
his own shadow
and wonders
why it is dark.

ZEN PROVERB

The person
who says it cannot
be done should
not interrupt the
person doing it.

Follow your inner moonlight; don't hide the madness.

ALLEN GINSBERG

Most of the time,
all you have is the
moment, and
the imperfect love
of the people
around you.

ANNE LAMOTT

Sometimes,
simply by sitting,
the soul collects
wisdom.

ZEN PROVERB

As a fletcher makes
straight his arrow,
a wise man makes
straight his trembling
and unsteady thought,
which is difficult to
guard and difficult
to hold back.

BUDDHA

Student of meditation:
"I feel distracted, or my
legs ache, or I fall asleep."
Teacher: "It will pass."
Student, a week later:
"I feel so aware,
so peaceful, so alive."
Teacher: "It will pass."

If you neglect your art for one day it will neglect you for two.

CHINESE PROVERB

Issan Dorsey
was asked,
"What is the essence
of Zen art?"
He replied,
"Nothing extra."

The bird of paradise lands only on the hand that does not grasp.

ZEN PROVERB

Think different.

Steve Jobs

Live in simple
faith . . .
Just as this
trusting cherry
Flowers, fades,
and falls.

Issa

In the stillness
of the mind I saw
myself as I am—
unbound.

Sri Nisargadatta Maharaj

All things in nature work silently. They come into being and possess nothing. They fulfill their functions and make no claim.

LAO TZU

Come, said
the Muse,
Sing me a song
no poet yet
has chanted.
Sing me the
Universal.

WALT WHITMAN

We have only
now, only this
single eternal
moment opening
and unfolding
before us, day
and night.

JACK KORNFIELD

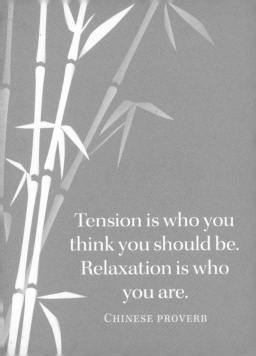

Tension is who you
think you should be.
Relaxation is who
you are.

CHINESE PROVERB

Give thanks
for unknown
blessings already
on their way.

NATIVE AMERICAN SAYING

Now the swinging bridge
Is quieted with creepers…
Like our tendrilled life.

BASHO

Awakened within a dream,
I fall into my own arms.
…What kept you so long?

LOU HARTMAN

This is the real secret
of life—to be completely
engaged with what you
are doing in the here and
now. And instead of
calling it work, realize
it is play.

ALAN WILSON WATTS

One can appreciate and celebrate each moment—there's nothing more sacred. There's nothing more vast or absolute. In fact, there's nothing more!

PEMA CHÖDRÖN

Yes, there is a Nirvana;
it is in leading your
sheep to a green
pasture, and in putting
your child to sleep,
and in writing the last
line of your poem.

KAHLIL GIBRAN

Supernatural
Cool breeze . . .
Buddha's paradise
Must lie thataway.

Issa

Smile, breathe, and go slowly.

Thích Nhất Hanh